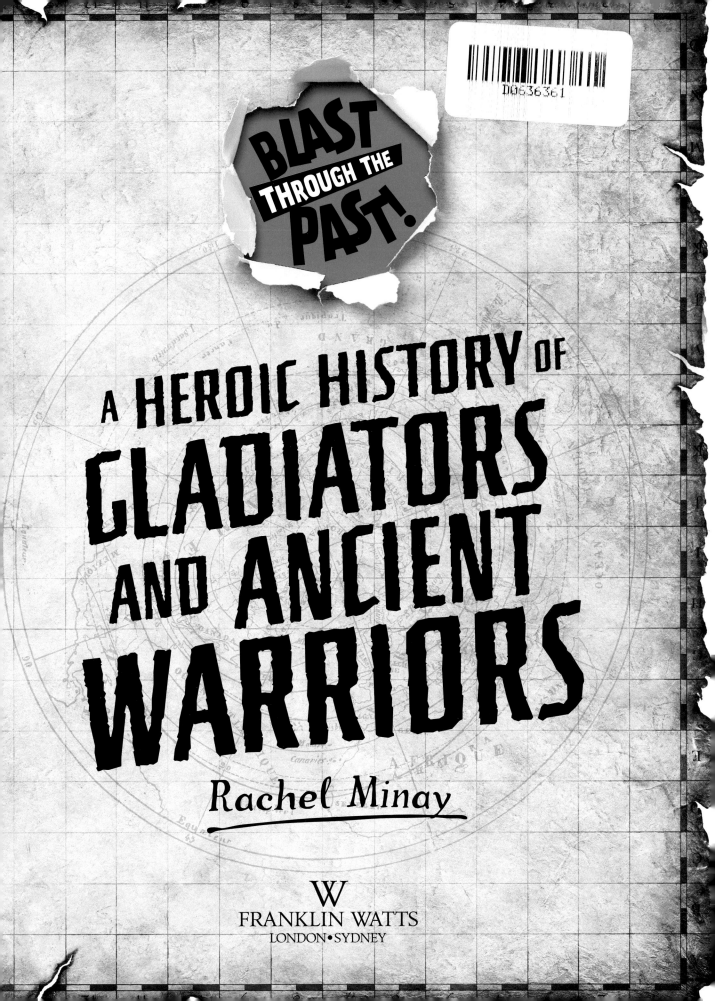

BLAST THROUGH THE PAST!

A HEROIC HISTORY OF GLADIATORS AND ANCIENT WARRIORS

Rachel Minay

W
FRANKLIN WATTS
LONDON · SYDNEY

Franklin Watts
First published in Great Britain in 2016 by The Watts Publishing Group

Produced for Franklin Watts by
White-Thomson Publishing Ltd
www.wtpub.co.uk

Credits
Series Editor: Izzi Howell
Series Designer: Rocket Design (East Anglia) Ltd
Series Consultant: Philip Parker

The publisher would like to thank the following for permission to reproduce their pictures:
Shutterstock/Kamira 6; Shutterstock/Krikkiat 7; Shutterstock/vagabond54 8; Alamy/Ivy Close
Images 9; Shutterstock/George W. Bailey 10t; Alamy/The Art Archive 10b; Shutterstock/
Anastasios71 11t; Shutterstock/Peter Hermes Furian 11b; Alamy/AF archive 12; Shutterstock/Panos
Karas 13; Wikimedia 14; Shutterstock/Hung Chung Chih 15l; Shutterstock/TonyV3112 15r; Peter
Dennis/Wayland 16l; Alamy/Heritage Image Partnership Ltd 16r; Corbis/Stapleton Collection 17l;
Wikimedia/Kabuto 7 17r; Shutterstock/Peter Hermes Furia 18; Shutterstock/Regien Paassen 19;
Shutterstock/CoolR 20; Shutterstock/Clara 21t; Alamy/Pictorial Press Ltd 21b; Alamy/AF archive
22; Corbis/Atlantide Phototravel 23t; Alamy/Glasshouse Images 23b; Corbis/Charles & Josette
Lenars 24t; Shutterstock/underworld 24b; Corbis 25; Alamy/North Wind Picture Archives 26;
Shutterstock/Catmando 27t; Wikimedia/Søren Niedziella 27b; Alamy/Steve Lindridge 28; istock/
AndrewJShearer 29. All design elements from Shutterstock.

Every attempt has been made to clear copyright. Should there be any inadvertent
omission please apply to the publisher for rectification.

ISBN 978 1 4451 4929 5

Printed in China

MIX
Paper from
responsible sources
FSC® C104740
www.fsc.org

Franklin Watts
An imprint of
Hachette Children's Group
Part of The Watts Publishing Group
Carmelite House
50 Victoria Embankment
London EC4Y 0DZ

An Hachette UK Company
www.hachette.co.uk

www.franklinwatts.co.uk

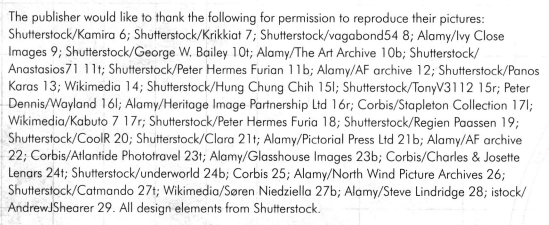

Words in **bold** appear in the glossary on pages 30 and 31.

CONTENTS

GLADIATORS AND ANCIENT WARRIORS THROUGH HISTORY

Throughout history, people have fought bitter wars to expand their own territory or to defend themselves against attack.

In ancient Rome, fighting was not just a way of life for the soldiers in the vast Roman army. Gladiators fought to the death for the entertainment of bloodthirsty crowds.

Discover what it was like to be a warrior at different moments in history. Read on to find out how the lives of these warriors changed over time.

Narmer
(Egypt) ●
reigned c. 3100 BCE

This timeline shows you the names, nationalities and dates of the people mentioned in this book.

ATLANTIC
OCEAN

SOUTH
AMERICA

Urged the Celts to rebel against Roman rule

Olaf
Tryggvason
(Norway) ○
c. CE 960s–1000

Shield Jaguar and Lady Xoc
(Yaxchilan, Maya city) ●
reigned CE 681–742

Boudicca
(Britain) ●
died c. CE 61

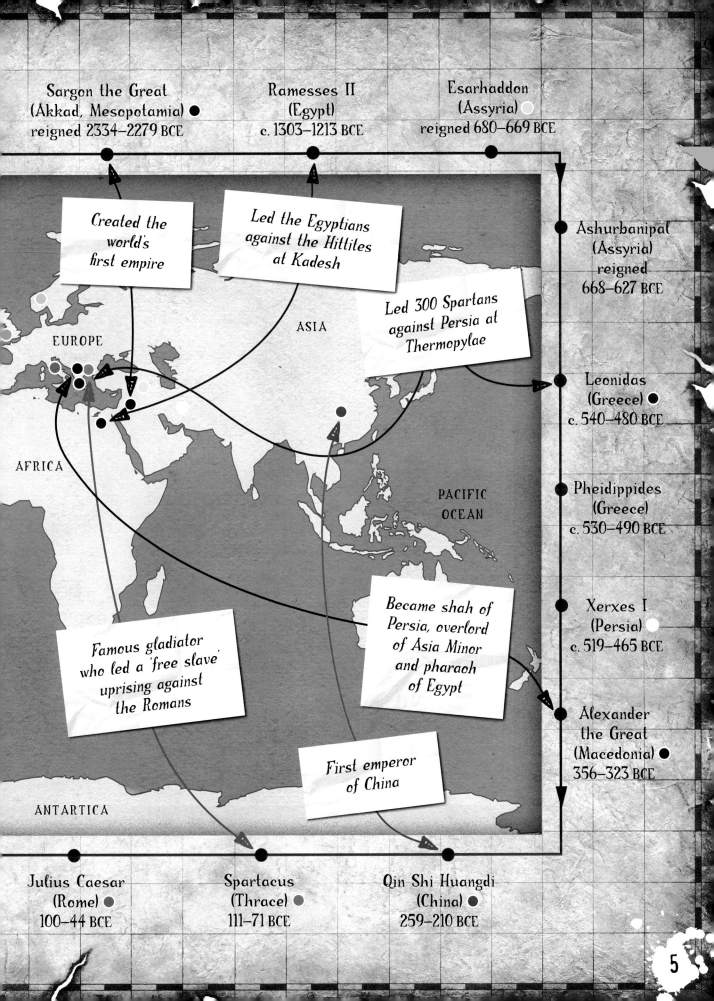

Sargon the Great
(Akkad, Mesopotamia) ●
reigned 2334–2279 BCE

Ramesses II
(Egypt)
c. 1303–1213 BCE

Esarhaddon
(Assyria)
reigned 680–669 BCE

Ashurbanipal
(Assyria)
reigned
668–627 BCE

Created the
world's
first empire

Led the Egyptians
against the Hittites
at Kadesh

Led 300 Spartans
against Persia at
Thermopylae

ASIA

EUROPE

AFRICA

Leonidas
(Greece) ●
c. 540–480 BCE

PACIFIC
OCEAN

Pheidippides
(Greece)
c. 530–490 BCE

Became shah of
Persia, overlord
of Asia Minor
and pharaoh
of Egypt

Xerxes I
(Persia)
c. 519–465 BCE

Famous gladiator
who led a 'free slave'
uprising against
the Romans

Alexander
the Great
(Macedonia) ●
356–323 BCE

First emperor
of China

ANTARTICA

Julius Caesar
(Rome) ●
100–44 BCE

Spartacus
(Thrace) ●
111–71 BCE

Qin Shi Huangdi
(China) ●
259–210 BCE

CLASHING CULTURES

The world's first civilisations grew up in **Mesopotamia** and included the **Sumerians**, Akkadians and **Assyrians**. Trade and wealth grew, and so did cities. This led to warfare and the first **empires**, as countries began to expand their own land by invading others.

War and peace

The Sumerians were fantastic farmers, clever craftspeople, terrific traders, used the wheel and invented writing! Sounds amazing, right? Well, Sargon the Great obviously thought so, because around 2334 BCE he began the conquest of Sumer, making it part of his Akkadian Empire.

WILD WARRIORS

NAME: Sargon the Great
NATIONALITY: Akkadian
AKA: Early empire-builder
ACHIEVEMENTS: Sargon created what some consider the world's first empire by ruling Akkad and conquering neighbouring Sumer.

This box from the ancient Sumerian city of Ur shows images of war and peace. 'Peace' shows a banquet with food and music. 'War' shows soldiers and chariots riding over enemies.

The warlike Assyrians started to build their vast empire from about 1000 BCE, defeating other kingdoms including the Babylonians and parts of Egypt.

Assyrians were particularly skilled at attacking cities: they surrounded them and then attacked the walls in three ways. They used ladders to climb over them, pioneered the use of **battering rams** to break them down and dug tunnels under to collapse them. Once captured, the people inside were taken prisoner, tortured or killed.

HAVE YOU GOT WHAT IT TAKES?
ASSYRIAN KING

PERSONALITY PROFILE: Lion tamer

In Assyria, only kings were allowed to hunt lions and the hunt was **symbolic** – it made kings look strong and able to protect their people.

HE SAID WHAT?

'I am powerful, I am **omnipotent**, I am a hero, I am gigantic, I am colossal.'

This is how one Assyrian king, Esarhaddon, described himself. No problems with self-esteem then!

The Assyrian king Ashurbanipal decorated his palace with pictures of him on a lion hunt.

Ashurbanipal

EPIC EGYPTIANS

As people settled along the rivers in Mesopotamia, another mighty civilisation was developing on the banks of the Nile in North Africa. Around 3100 BCE, the first warrior **pharaoh**, probably called Narmer, made Egypt into one kingdom.

Weapons of war

Ancient **Egyptian** weapons included bows and arrows, axes, **maces**, spears and a sword with a 'sickle' or curved blade, called a khopesh. Early weapons were made from wood and stone or **obsidian**; later ones were made from bronze and then iron.

This ancient Egyptian wall painting shows soldiers carrying a variety of weapons.

Axe

Spear

I'd A [WI ['I want an axe next time!

Khopesh

Shield

WILD WARRIORS

NAME: Ramesses II

NATIONALITY: Egyptian

KNOWN FOR: Military might

ACHIEVEMENTS: Ramesses II was a great military ruler who led campaigns against the Nubians (to the south of Egypt) and the Hittites (who lived in what is now Turkey).

Pictures of the Battle of Kadesh often show Ramesses II fighting beside his pet lion!

Run, lads!

Warfare changed around 1648 BCE, when people called the Hyksos invaded. Egyptian foot soldiers were no match for the enemy's horses and chariots.

In time, the Egyptians developed their own chariot and used it to force the Hyksos out and fight others, such as the warlike Hittites. Ramesses II led Egypt against the Hittites at the Battle of Kadesh in 1274 BCE. With over 5,000 chariots involved, it may have been the biggest chariot battle in history.

HAVE YOU GOT WHAT IT TAKES?
FOOT SOLDIER

PERSONALITY PROFILE:
Fighting farmer

To begin with, Egypt didn't have an organised army. In times of war, the pharaoh would call up ordinary farmers to fight as infantry (foot soldiers). They had a shield for protection, but not much armour and no shoes.

GLORIOUS GREEKS

The ancient **Greeks** were amazing architects, pioneers in politics and invented the Olympic Games. They weren't all about art and culture, though! The argumentative **city-states** often fought each other, but their main enemy was **Persia**.

Get in line!

Hoplites were Greek foot soldiers. Although they were ordinary people rather than professional soldiers, they were effective because they used a **phalanx** formation. Protecting one another with their wall of shields, the hoplites fought the enemy with long spears.

HAVE YOU GOT WHAT IT TAKES?
TROJAN-TRICKER

TOP SKILL: Lying low

Sshh! Don't let the **Trojans** know you're here! Legend has it that early Greek warriors called the Mycenaeans hid inside a great wooden horse to sneak in and attack the city of Troy.

This 7th-century jug shows hoplites fighting in lines.

HAVE YOU GOT WHAT IT TAKES?
* MARATHON RUNNER *

PERSONALITY PROFILE:
Galloping Greek

It's 490 BCE and it's Athens v Persia in the Battle of Marathon. Could you run 250 km to ask for help (you won't get it), then fight in a battle, then run 40 km to Athens to tell them you've won? A Greek called Pheidippides is said to have done just that – unfortunately he died when he arrived!

The **trireme** was a fast Greek warship that could smash holes in enemy boats. The Greeks won a famous sea battle at Salamis, near Athens, when they trapped the much bigger Persian fleet and then sank it.

So did the Greeks conquer Persia in the end? In fact, a man from Macedonia (a kingdom in the northeast of Greece) did ...

How great am I?

Alexander's empire

WILD ⚔ WARRIORS

NAME: Alexander the Great
NATIONALITY: Macedonian
AKA: Undefeated military genius
ACHIEVEMENTS: By the age of twenty-five he was king of Macedonia, pharaoh of Egypt, overlord of Asia Minor and great king of Persia. He never lost a single battle.

HE SAID WHAT?

'There is nothing impossible to him who will try.'

Alexander had well-trained, loyal troops and introduced lighter armour and longer spears. His success was also due to his determination, quick understanding and skill in spotting decisive moments in battle.

SPECTACULAR SPARTANS

Sparta was a Greek city~state of professional fighters. Time to toughen up!

Fighting fit

Spartan warriors had a fearsome reputation, not that surprising considering they were born and bred to fight. Between the ages of seven and thirty, male Spartans lived in barracks, undertaking hard training and becoming full soldiers at the age of twenty.

HAVE YOU GOT WHAT IT TAKES?
SPARTAN CHILD

PERSONALITY PROFILE: Tough nut

First, think yourself lucky if you get to childhood – weak Spartan babies were left to die. Boys had to leave home aged seven to learn how to fight; girls learned wrestling and racing so they grew up strong.

Like other Greeks, Spartan hoplites also used a phalanx formation.

The Spartans' greatest moment came in 480 BCE. The vast Persian army was trying to invade and conquer Greece, but strong phalanxes were blocking the narrow pass at Thermopylae and beating the Persian attack.

However, one Greek betrayed the others, telling the Persian king, Xerxes, how to get around the pass. The Spartan king Leonidas, along with just 300 Spartans and a few hundred others, stayed to fight. Eventually defeated, 'the 300' held off the enemy for as long as possible fighting with everything they had — even their hands and teeth — so the other Greeks could escape.

WILD WARRIORS

NAME: Leonidas

NATIONALITY: Spartan

AKA: Fearless fighter

ACHIEVEMENTS: Eventually killed at the Battle of Thermopylae, Leonidas was the typical heroic Spartan king, who inspired his men to die fighting rather than ever surrender.

This statue of Leonidas stands in the present-day city of Sparta.

MUST BE ABLE TO:
remember your shield

Spartans who died in battle were carried home on their shields. Tough Spartan mothers were said to say to their sons, 'Come back with your shield, or on it.'

CHINA'S TERRACOTTA ARMY

During the Warring States period (475–221 BCE), different regions struggled to control the vast area that became ancient China. The **Qin** eventually beat the other warring states and their leader, Qin Shi Huangdi, left an incredible legacy.

Thousands of warriors

Qin Shi Huangdi had a fear of death and spent a lot of time looking for an **elixir of life**. Unsurprisingly, he didn't find one, but he had the next best thing: he was buried with about 8,000 terracotta (clay) soldiers to protect him in the afterlife. Apparently he started planning this soon after taking the throne at the age of thirteen – that's thinking ahead!

Clay

Qin Shi Huangdi became the first emperor of China in 221 BCE.

14

The Terracotta Army also tells us about real Qin warriors. We know they fought with armed infantry and chariots surrounded by many powerful archers. The crossbow was a deadly weapon, but designed so someone could learn to use it quickly. This explains how an army made up of Qin peasants managed to defeat all others and founded the country now known as China.

Each terracotta warrior is lifesize and no two are exactly the same.

The warriors were originally painted in bright colours, but as they were excavated the paint started to curl in 15 seconds and flake off in just four minutes.

COURAGEOUS CELTS

The **Celts** were not one nation, but different groups who shared similar ways of life. Powerful Celtic tribes grew up during the Iron Age (around 800 BCE~CE 50) and settled across Europe.

Celtic warriors carried oval, round or long rectangular shields.

Fierce fighters

What's that blood~curdling noise? Who are those blue people with strange, spiky hair charging towards you throwing spears and brandishing swords? Wait a minute ... some of those people appear to be naked!

This is what it might have felt like to be an enemy of the Celts. Warriors sometimes painted their bodies blue and used lime to spike their hair. They often fought wearing nothing but a **torc** round the neck, which the Celts believed had a mystical power and gave them special protection in battle.

A torc was a metal ring that usually had a gap at the front.

Celtic warriors fought on foot, on horseback and used chariots. They carried heavy iron swords and sharp bronze spears. Other than a shield, they might only wear a helmet for protection.

Not all Celtic warriors were men – women also fought in some big battles. One woman has become famous for leading her Celtic tribe, the Iceni, in battle – Queen Boudicca.

Toooot

MUST BE ABLE TO:
play the carnyx

The carnyx (war trumpet) was a Celtic wind instrument with an end shaped like an animal's head. Blown in battle, it made a deafening din to terrify the enemy.

WILD ⚜ WARRIORS

NAME: Boudicca

NATIONALITY: Briton and Celt

AKA: Courageous queen who led an anti-Roman rebellion in CE 61

ACHIEVEMENTS: Boudicca led a violent uprising against Roman rule, destroying Colchester, London and St Albans.

SHE SAID WHAT?

'On this spot we must either conquer, or die with glory.'

The Romans finally crushed the rebellion, but it's thought Boudicca poisoned herself rather than be taken prisoner.

REMARKABLE ROMANS

The Romans were one of the most powerful civilisations ever, due in large part to their massive and well-trained army. By CE 117, they had expanded into most of modern Europe, as well as parts of the Middle East and North Africa.

No cowards allowed

The Roman army was made up of **legionaries**, who were always Roman **citizens**, and **auxiliaries**. Auxiliaries often came from other parts of the empire and had unique skills. For example, the Numidians from North Africa were outstanding on horseback, and the Cretans and Syrians were famed for their archery.

HAVE YOU GOT WHAT IT TAKES?
LEGIONARY

TOP SKILLS: Marching and endurance

The Roman Empire was colossal (see map) so soldiers often fought far from home. Skilled and highly organised, soldiers could march over 50 km a day, build a camp each night and then move on in the morning.

The Roman Empire in CE 117, at its greatest extent

Rome

Lazy soldiers were beaten, and trying to avoid joining the army or running away meant a death sentence. Decimation was a cruel and terrifying punishment for cowardly behaviour by a group of soldiers who tried to **desert** or rebel. The men were lined up and one in ten was brutally killed.

MUST BE ABLE TO:
handle siege weapons

The Romans were excellent at **siege** warfare. Their two top siege weapons were the onager, a catapult that could fire burning rocks, and the ballista, a powerful crossbow that could automatically fire iron-tipped arrows.

Roman soldiers protected each other by holding their shields to make a 'tortoise' shape.

WILD 🦁 WARRIORS

NAME: Julius Caesar

NATIONALITY: Roman

AKA: The Roman geezer

ACHIEVEMENTS: Caesar was a superb leader who lived at the time just before the rise of the Roman Empire. His ruthless ambition made him many enemies and he was assassinated in CE 44.

HE SAID WHAT?

'I came, I saw, I conquered.'

Or, as Caesar would have written it in Latin, '*Veni, vidi, vici*'. This was the simple but powerful way he described one of his victories to the people back in Rome.

GLADIATORS GALORE!

Have you ever been to a big stadium to watch a sports event or music concert? The Romans enjoyed massive events like these too, but they had much gorier spectacles – gladiator fights.

Gory glory

Gladiators were usually men, but there were a few female gladiators. They were often slaves, criminals or **prisoners of war** who were forced to fight. Like modern sports stars, a good gladiator could become rich and famous. The downside? Most of them were killed long before they gained celebrity status.

HAVE YOU GOT WHAT IT TAKES?
GLADIATOR

PERSONALITY PROFILE:
Dude with a death wish?

Young men joined the ludus (gladiator school) at about seventeen. Some were volunteers, but many were forced to join and then guarded so they didn't escape. New recruits had to agree to being burned, chained and beaten in training – and to being killed in the ring!

Gladiators fought in huge **amphitheatres** like this one, the Colosseum in Rome.

Gladiator fights sometimes had a theme, for example the floor of the Colosseum in Rome could be flooded for 'sea battles'. An amazing variety of wild animals were brought to be killed in the ring, including tigers, bears, elephants and even crocodiles.

Both gladiators and exotic animals were brought from the far reaches of the empire to fight.

MUST BE ABLE TO:

use a gladius

Gladiators got their name from the gladius (a short sword), but gladiators used different weapons and armour. One style used a **trident** and a net to entangle the opponent.

Oi, do you mind?

Trident

Net

Gladius

SPLENDID SPARTACUS

The best-known gladiator of all may have started out tending lambs, but ended up a legend – Spartacus.

Gosh, I'm in BIG trouble!

Who was Spartacus?

Born in Thrace (now Bulgaria), Spartacus probably started life as a shepherd. It's thought he then worked as a Roman soldier, but deserted. Desertion wasn't popular with the Romans; they caught him and sold him into slavery. He was bought by a gladiator trainer and forced to join the ludus. Ever the rebel, Spartacus broke out, setting fire to the ludus as he left.

He was in BIG trouble with the Romans now!

Kirk Douglas played the title role in the 1960 film Spartacus.

Where could he hide? Well, the obvious place would be in the crater of a volcano, wouldn't it? Spartacus and his followers looted from rich Romans and freed their slaves, who they then trained to fight.

The Romans kept setting out to fight Spartacus's 'free slave army' – which may have grown to about 100,000 – but kept being beaten. Eventually, Spartacus was killed in battle and 6,000 of his followers were **crucified** as an example to other slaves.

Can you turn the heating down?

Spartacus hid on Mt Vesuvius! He was lucky – about 100 years later (in CE 79) the same volcano erupted.

WILD WARRIORS

NAME: Spartacus

NATIONALITY: Thracian

AKA: Fave slave saver

ACHIEVEMENTS: Leading a rebel army against the Romans – and nearly beating them. As a former gladiator, he must have been brave, strong and quick-thinking. As a former slave, he must have been inspirational to his followers.

Spartacus died in 71 BCE but has gone down in history as a symbol of fighting for freedom.

MIGHTY MAYA

The **Maya** lived around the same time as the Celts and the Romans, but on the other side of the world in the rainforests of Central America. The different Maya kingdoms were sometimes trading partners and often at war.

Ruling the rainforest

Maya warriors might wear padded cotton armour that was stiffened with salt or just a **loincloth**. Sometimes they wore feather headdresses and jaguar skins.

Weapons were made from stone (such as obsidian) and wood, and included spears, knives, bows and arrows. Warriors only fought during the day and called a **truce** at night.

This wall painting shows a Mayan battle scene.

The Maya built incredible stone pyramids and created paintings and sculptures.

Bedtime juice?

Fight you again in the morning!

Battles carried on until the leader of one side was killed. Then the losing side had to pay a tribute (which could be people, gold, silver, goods or even salt) to the winner.

The Maya believed they had to make blood sacrifices to please their gods. They would sacrifice animals and sometimes people – usually slaves or prisoners from other cities.

The Maya were at their most powerful from about CE 250. But 700 years later, most of their cities were deserted and in ruins. No one knows what happened to the once-mighty rulers of the rainforest.

Blood sacrifice wasn't just for slaves and captives. This carving shows a Maya queen making a blood offering by pulling a thorny string through her tongue. Ouch!

MUST BE ABLE TO:

grow chillies

The Maya didn't just use the spicy chilli to flavour their food; they may have used it as a weapon. Burning stacks of chillies would make a powerful smokescreen – now that's eye-watering!

King Shield Jaguar

Lady Xoc

VOYAGING VIKINGS

The **Vikings** came from Scandinavia (Denmark, Norway and Sweden). Between CE 800 and 1066, these ruthless raiders travelled far, looking for new land and treasure to steal.

Pirate raiders

Vikings settled in Britain, founded Normandy (which means 'Land of the North Men') in France and travelled to the Mediterranean, Russia and even North America. They weren't all peaceful settlers though! Vikings were terrifying warriors who stole treasures from churches and monastaries, took prisoners and burned buildings. In fact, the word 'Viking' means 'a pirate raid' in the Old Norse language.

Put me down!

This print shows the king of Norway, Olaf Tryggvason, leading a raid on England in the late 900s.

You're looking out across the sea. What's that mysterious shape on the horizon? Eek! It's a Viking longship! These boats were fast and sneaky, could sail up rivers and launch surprise attacks. Powered by both sails and oars, the biggest longships could carry 70 rowers, horses and many warriors.

A frightening figurehead, such as a dragon, at the front of a ship let any onlookers know the Vikings weren't out for a pleasure cruise …

Typical Viking weapons were spears, axes and swords. Some Vikings could throw two spears at once or even catch a spear that was thrown at them, only to launch it back at the enemy. Battle axes were heavy weapons that could be single or double handed. Viking swords were made from iron, or in later years, steel, which made a strong, sharp blade.

MUST BE ABLE TO:

name your sword

Vikings were very fond of their swords, often passing them down through families and giving them names like 'Gold-hilt', 'Leg biter' and 'Adder'.

VICTORIOUS VIKINGS

The Vikings liked to play hard and fight hard. An intimidating enemy, they were strong, fierce and sometimes charged into battle howling like wolves!

Gruesome games

Viking warriors were pretty angry even when they were relaxing. 'Downtime' included wrestling for both men and women, fencing, knife juggling and sometimes deadly swimming contests.

Berserker

This 12th-century chess set features a wild-eyed berserker biting his shield.

Battles and burial

Vikings believed that when a battle began, the Norse god Odin sent out female warrior spirits called valkyries who decided who would live and who would die. Those who died in battle would go to Valhalla, a hall in the afterlife lined with gold spears and shields.

People from the Shetland Islands, Scotland, celebrate their Viking heritage by burning a longship at this annual festival.

stomach onion porridge

Wounded warriors were served up onion porridge and then sniffed by other Vikings. If they smelled of onions, the wound had probably gone through to the stomach, which would most likely be fatal. (It also meant their last meal was onion porridge. Talk about bad luck!)

Yuk!

When a Viking died, their body was usually burned. Their loved ones believed that a hot fire with lots of smoke made it easier for the dead person to reach Valhalla. The most spectacular funerals were reserved for chieftains and the greatest Viking warriors. The dead warrior would be buried with their longship – either on land or set alight and put out to sea.

GLOSSARY

BCE – the letters BCE stand for 'before common era'. They refer to dates before the year CE 1.

CE – the letters CE stand for 'common era'. They refer to dates after the year CE 1.

amphitheatre – a round building without a roof, used for sports or other entertainment

auxiliary – a soldier in the Roman army who was not a citizen

battering ram – a long iron-tipped wooden trunk used to break down walls

citizen – in ancient Rome, a Roman man who was allowed to vote in elections and be a legionary

city-state – in ancient Greece, an independent area based around a city or an island; the city-states all had their own rules and ways of life

crucify – kill by hanging on a cross

desert – leave the army without permission

dynasty – a line of rulers from the same family

elixir of life – a mythical potion that supposedly gives the drinker everlasting life

empire – a group of countries under the control of one country

excavate – uncover something that is buried in the ground

hoplite – an armed foot soldier in ancient Greece

legionary – a Roman soldier; there were about 5,000 legionaries in a legion

loincloth – a piece of cloth worn around the hips

mace – a heavy club

Mesopotamia – an ancient region between the Tigris and Euphrates rivers (largely modern-day Iraq but including parts of Syria and Turkey)

obsidian – a hard, black, glassy stone that is made when volcanoes erupt

omnipotent – all-powerful

phalanx – in ancient Greece, a group of soldiers armed with shields and spears who marched and fought in a rectangular formation

pharaoh – the ruler of ancient Egypt

prisoner of war – someone captured by the enemy in a war

siege – attack on a city or fort by surrounding it

symbolic – where one thing stands for something else

torc – a ring made from gold, silver or bronze that Celts wore around their necks

trident – a three-pronged spear

trireme – an ancient Greek warship powered by three rows of oars

Trojan – a person from ancient Troy, a legendary city involved in the story of the Trojan War. Some historians now believe Troy may have been a real city.

truce – an agreement to stop fighting for a certain length of time

ANCIENT CIVILISATIONS

SUMERIANS
(3500–2300 BCE) – an ancient civilisation from southern Mesopotamia, credited with the invention of writing.

ASSYRIANS
(2600–612 BCE) – a warlike civilisation from northern Mesopotamia whose warrior kings began to build an empire from around 1000 BCE.

EGYPTIANS
(3100–30 BCE) – a civilisation based around the River Nile in Egypt, which was ruled by a pharaoh.

GREEKS
(750–30 BCE) – an advanced Mediterranean civilisation that studied science, maths and medicine.

VIKINGS
(CE 700–1100) – a group of people originally from Scandinavia that conquered land across northern Europe and the north Atlantic, creating a Viking empire.

- Vikings
- Egyptians
- Greeks
- Sumerians
- Assyrians
- Persians
- Qin Dynasty
- Celts
- Maya

CELTS
(c. 800 BCE–CE 50) – a group of peoples who lived across Europe, spoke Celtic languages and shared a similar culture.

MAYA
(c. 250 BCE–CE 900) – a civilisation that developed over what is now southern Mexico, Guatemala and Belize, and had a sophisticated writing system and calendar.

PERSIANS
(c. 550–330 BCE) – the first Persian empire was founded by Cyrus the Great (reigned 559–530 BCE) and eventually conquered by Alexander the Great.

QIN DYNASTY
(221–206 BCE) – although it did not last very long, the Qin Dynasty is important because it was the first dynasty of a united China.

INDEX

Further information

http://www.bbc.co.uk/schools/primaryhistory/

Follow the links to discover ancient Greek, Roman and Viking warfare.

http://www.bbc.co.uk/history/ancient/romans/launch_gms_gladiator.shtml

Choose your gladiator's weapons and armour in this 'Dressed to Kill' game.

http://ancienthistory.mrdonn.org/index.html

Find out more about ancient civilisations, including Mesopotamia, China, the Celts and the Maya.